AI-driven Innovations in Robotic Engineering

Automation

Beyond Automation: Navigating Tomorrow's Frontiers with AI-Infused Robotics

JAMES BRANDY

TABLE OF CONTENTS

INTRODUCTION

In the tapestry of technological progress, the symphony of artificial intelligence (AI) harmonizes seamlessly with the precision of robotic engineering, weaving a narrative of unparalleled innovation. Welcome to the pages of "AI-driven Innovations in Robotic Engineering: Revolutionizing Automation for Tomorrow's World." In this groundbreaking exploration, we embark on a journey through the corridors of cutting-edge advancements, where AI and robotics converge to redefine the very fabric of our automated future.

As we traverse the realms of this transformative alliance, the chapters unfold to reveal the foundational principles underpinning AI and robotic synergy. From the early whispers of historical breakthroughs to the resounding crescendo of contemporary applications, we decipher the evolutionary path that has led us to the dawn of a new era. We aim to illuminate the landscape where smart machines, guided by the prowess of artificial intelligence, shape industries, reshape workforces, and reimagine the possibilities that lie ahead.

The present moment finds us at the nexus of limitless potential and ethical contemplation. Through the lens of real-world case studies, we navigate the diverse applications of AI in robotics, probing the challenges and opportunities that define this dynamic landscape. From healthcare to manufacturing, from autonomous vehicles to collaborative robotics, each chapter serves as a portal into the realms of innovation that are propelling us into an era where machines not only mimic human intelligence but augment it.

Yet, as we revel in the marvels of this technological revolution, we do not shy away from the responsibility it carries. Ethics becomes our guiding star as we explore the implications of AI-driven robotic systems on society, ushering in a dialogue on responsible innovation. This book strives to be a compass for decision-makers, engineers, researchers, and enthusiasts navigating the uncharted territories of a world where AI and robotics forge a profound partnership.

In the chapters that follow, we will dissect the algorithms, techniques, and collaborative landscapes that form the backbone of this revolution. With an eye toward the future, we will unravel the tapestry of possibilities that await, heralding a smarter, more interconnected, and automated tomorrow.

So, dear reader, fasten your seatbelts as we embark on a voyage through the realms of AI-driven innovations in robotic engineering, where the present meets the future, and the future is shaped by the ingenuity of today.

CHAPTER ONE

Foundations of AI and Robotics

1.1 Background and Context

The inception of the symbiotic relationship between artificial intelligence (AI) and robotics finds its roots in a historical continuum of technological evolution. To truly grasp the significance of their integration, it is essential to explore the background and context that have shaped these disciplines. From early automata to the first inklings of machine learning, this section unravels the historical tapestry, illuminating the pivotal moments that have led us to the current era of AI-driven innovations in robotic engineering. Understanding the contextual landscape not only provides insight into the challenges overcome but also sets the stage for envisioning the possibilities that lie ahead.

1.2 The Rise of AI in Robotics

The narrative of the rise of AI in robotics is a captivating journey through breakthroughs and innovations that have propelled technology beyond traditional boundaries. From the theoretical foundations laid by Alan Turing to the practical applications of neural networks, this chapter examines the ascent of artificial intelligence within the realm of robotics. We delve into key milestones, such as the birth of expert systems, the advent of machine learning algorithms, and the dawn of deep learning. By tracing this upward trajectory, we aim to elucidate how AI has become an integral force, reshaping the capabilities and potential of robotic systems.

1.3 Purpose and Scope of the Book

As we embark on this exploration of AI-driven innovations in robotic engineering, it is crucial to delineate the purpose and scope that guide our inquiry. This book seeks to provide a comprehensive understanding of the dynamic interplay between AI and robotics, offering insights into their historical foundations, current applications, and future trajectories. The purpose is not merely to chronicle the evolution but to illuminate the transformative impact on industries, societies, and the very fabric of our daily lives. The scope encompasses the examination of AI algorithms, real-world case studies, ethical considerations, and collaborative possibilities, providing readers with a holistic perspective on the revolutionizing force that is automation driven by artificial intelligence. Through this lens, we invite readers to join us on a journey through the past, present, and future of AI-driven innovations in robotic engineering.

CHAPTER TWO

Foundations of AI in Robotic Engineering

2.1 Understanding Artificial Intelligence

Artificial Intelligence (AI) serves as the cornerstone of innovation in the realm of robotic engineering. This section embarks on a comprehensive exploration of the fundamental principles that underpin AI. From classical rule-based systems to the complexities of machine learning and neural networks, we delve into the diverse facets of AI. Concepts such as natural language processing, computer vision, and decision-making algorithms are unraveled to provide readers with a nuanced understanding of the intelligence driving the robotic revolution. Through this, we lay the groundwork for the subsequent discussion on the integration of AI in robotic systems.

2.2 Robotics and Automation Overview

To comprehend the synergy between AI and robotics, a solid understanding of the foundations of robotics is paramount. This section provides an overview of robotics and automation, tracing their evolution from early industrial automation to the sophisticated robotic systems of today. We explore the key components of robotic engineering, including sensors, actuators, and control systems. Through an examination of the historical milestones and technological advancements, readers gain insight into the multifaceted nature of robotics, setting the stage for the convergence with AI.

2.3 Synergy between AI and Robotics

The fusion of AI and robotics marks a paradigm shift in automation. This section examines the intricate synergy between AI and robotics, highlighting how intelligent systems enhance the capabilities of robots. We explore how AI algorithms enable robots to adapt, learn, and make decisions in dynamic environments. Real-world examples and case studies showcase the transformative impact of this synergy across various industries. As we delve into collaborative robotics, where humans and AI-driven machines work hand in hand, we witness the emergence of a new era in automation. This chapter aims to provide readers with a solid foundation, laying the groundwork for a deeper exploration into the applications, challenges, and ethical considerations that define the landscape of AI-driven innovations in robotic engineering.

CHATER THREE

Evolution of AI in Robotics

3.1 Historical Milestones

Embarking on a journey through time, this section delves into the historical milestones that have defined the evolution of AI in robotics. From the conceptual foundations laid by early visionaries to the tangible breakthroughs that shaped the landscape, we explore pivotal moments that mark the convergence of artificial intelligence and robotic engineering. Historical milestones provide not only a chronological narrative but also insights into the challenges overcome and the foresight that has propelled us into the era of AI-driven innovations.

3.2 Technological Advancements

The evolution of AI in robotics is intrinsically linked to the rapid pace of technological advancements. This section unpacks the technological leaps that have propelled the field forward. From the advent of computing power to the refinement of algorithms, we scrutinize the tools and technologies that have fueled the development of intelligent robotic systems. Machine learning algorithms, computational capabilities, and breakthroughs in sensing technologies have collectively contributed to the evolution, enabling robots to perceive, learn, and adapt in ways previously deemed improbable.

3.3 Key Developments Shaping the Field

In the dynamic interplay between AI and robotics, key developments continually reshape the landscape. This section focuses on contemporary trends and emerging paradigms that are shaping the future of AI-driven robotic engineering. We explore developments in areas such as swarm robotics, explainable AI, and the fusion of AI with other disruptive technologies. By examining the forefront of research and innovation, readers gain insights into the ongoing transformations and the potential trajectories that lie ahead. This chapter serves as a bridge between the historical foundations and the cutting-edge advancements, offering a panoramic view of the evolutionary tapestry weaving AI and robotics together.

CHAPTER FOUR

Current State of AI in Robotic Engineering

4.1 Case Studies of AI-Driven Robotics

This section takes a close look at the practical applications of AI in robotics through in-depth case studies. By examining real-world examples, readers gain valuable insights into how AI-driven robotic systems are functioning across various domains. From healthcare and manufacturing to service industries and beyond, we delve into the intricacies of successful implementations. These case studies not only showcase the capabilities of AI in enhancing robotic performance but also highlight the diversity of applications that are currently reshaping industries.

4.2 Industry Applications and Implementations

Building upon the case studies, this section explores the broader spectrum of industry applications and implementations of AI in robotic engineering. We analyze how different sectors, from automotive and aerospace to agriculture and logistics, are integrating AI-driven robotics into their workflows. The focus is on understanding the specific challenges these industries face and the tailored solutions that AI provides. By illuminating the varied applications, readers gain a comprehensive view of the transformative impact AI is having on the industrial landscape.

4.3 Challenges and Opportunities

In navigating the current state of AI in robotic engineering, it is imperative to address the challenges and opportunities that arise. This section critically examines the hurdles faced in deploying AI-driven robotic systems, including issues of reliability, safety, and ethical considerations. Simultaneously, we explore the myriad opportunities that arise from overcoming these challenges. The chapter concludes with a forward-looking perspective, highlighting the potential avenues for growth, innovation, and the societal impact of AI-driven robotic engineering. By comprehensively assessing the current landscape, this chapter serves as a bridge between the practical applications of today and the possibilities that lie on the horizon.

5.1 Machine Learning in Robotics

Machine learning stands as a cornerstone in the arsenal of AI techniques transforming robotic engineering. This section delves into the diverse applications of machine learning in robotics. From classic supervised learning for image recognition to unsupervised learning for pattern detection, we explore how machine learning algorithms empower robots to learn from data and adapt to dynamic environments. Case studies and practical examples illustrate the versatility of machine learning, showcasing its pivotal role in enhancing the cognitive capabilities of robotic systems.

5.2 Deep Learning Applications

Deep learning, with its neural network architectures, has revolutionized the field of AI and, by extension, robotics. In this section, we unravel the applications of deep learning in the realm of robotics. From convolutional neural networks (CNNs) for image processing to recurrent neural networks (RNNs) for sequential decision-making, we explore how deep learning algorithms enable robots to achieve unprecedented levels of perception and decision-making. The chapter delves into cutting-edge developments, illustrating how deep learning is reshaping the landscape of AI-driven robotic engineering.

5.3 Reinforcement Learning in Robotic Systems

Reinforcement learning introduces a paradigm where robots learn through interaction with their environment. This section illuminates the principles of reinforcement learning and its applications in robotic systems. From training robotic arms to perform intricate tasks to optimizing the navigation of autonomous vehicles, we explore how reinforcement learning algorithms enable robots to learn from trial and error, adapting their behavior based on feedback. Case studies exemplify the dynamic capabilities of reinforcement learning, showcasing its potential to drive autonomous decision-making and skill acquisition in diverse robotic applications.

By dissecting these key AI algorithms and techniques, this chapter provides readers with a comprehensive understanding of the technological underpinnings that empower robots to learn, reason, and act in increasingly sophisticated ways.

CHAPTER SIX

Integration of AI and Robotics: Case Studies

6.1 Healthcare Robotics

In the realm of healthcare, the integration of AI and robotics is reshaping diagnostics, treatment, and patient care. This section explores case studies where robotic systems, enhanced by artificial intelligence, are revolutionizing healthcare delivery. From surgical robots with enhanced precision to robotic assistants aiding in patient care, we delve into the transformative impact of AI-driven robotics in the medical field. Real-world examples showcase how these technologies are improving patient outcomes, increasing efficiency, and expanding the boundaries of what is possible in healthcare robotics.

6.2 Manufacturing and Industry 4.0

The manufacturing sector is at the forefront of the Industry 4.0 revolution, leveraging AI-driven robotics to optimize production processes. This section examines case studies that exemplify the integration of AI and robotics in manufacturing. From robotic arms collaborating with human workers to fully autonomous production lines, we explore how intelligent automation is enhancing efficiency, reducing costs, and driving innovation in the manufacturing industry. These case studies provide insights into the diverse applications of AI-driven robotics in the context of Industry 4.0.

6.3 Autonomous Vehicles and Drones

The integration of AI and robotics has paved the way for significant advancements in autonomous vehicles and drones. In this section, we delve into case studies that illustrate how AI is enabling self-driving cars, unmanned aerial vehicles, and other autonomous systems. From navigation algorithms that adapt to changing environments to real-time decision-making processes, we explore the intricate synergy between AI and robotics in the domain of transportation. These case studies offer a glimpse into the future of mobility, showcasing the potential of AI-driven robotics to revolutionize the way we move and transport goods.

This chapter illuminates the diverse applications of AI-driven robotics through concrete case studies in healthcare, manufacturing, and transportation. By examining real-world examples, readers gain a deeper understanding of how these technologies are making a tangible impact across different industries, heralding a new era of automation and intelligent systems.

CHAPTER SEVEN

Ethical Considerations in AI-Enhanced Robotics

7.1 Responsible AI Practices

As AI becomes an integral part of robotic engineering, ethical considerations take center stage. This section explores the principles of responsible AI practices in the context of robotics. From ensuring fairness in algorithmic decision-making to addressing biases in training data, we delve into the ethical dimensions of creating intelligent robotic systems. Case studies and best practices highlight how responsible AI practices can be integrated into the development and deployment of AI-enhanced robotics, fostering transparency and accountability.

7.2 Ensuring Transparency and Accountability

Transparency and accountability are paramount in the ethical deployment of AI-enhanced robotics. In this section, we examine strategies to ensure transparency throughout the lifecycle of robotic systems. From disclosing the decision-making processes of AI algorithms to establishing accountability frameworks for autonomous robots, we explore how openness can mitigate risks and build trust. Real-world examples illustrate the challenges and successes in implementing transparent and accountable practices in the development and deployment of AI-driven robotic systems.

7.3 Societal Impacts and Considerations

The societal impact of AI-enhanced robotics extends beyond technical considerations. This section delves into the broader implications and considerations for society at large. How do these technologies affect employment? What are the socio-economic implications of widespread automation? We explore these questions and more, aiming to foster a deeper understanding of the ethical responsibilities associated with the integration of AI in robotics. By examining the societal impacts, we aim to contribute to a thoughtful and informed discussion on the ethical considerations that should guide the development and deployment of AI-enhanced robotic systems.

This chapter serves as a critical exploration of the ethical dimensions surrounding AI-enhanced robotics, emphasizing the importance of responsible practices, transparency, and societal considerations. As we navigate the ethical landscape, the goal is to contribute to the establishment of guidelines and frameworks that ensure the ethical deployment of AI in robotic engineering.

CHAPTER EIGHT

Future Trends and Emerging Technologies

8.1 AI and the Next Frontier in Robotics

The future of robotics is intricately tied to the evolution of artificial intelligence. In this section, we explore the next frontier where AI is poised to take robotics to new heights. From advancements in cognitive computing to the integration of AI with other disruptive technologies, we analyze how intelligent systems are evolving and what lies ahead for the field of robotic engineering. By anticipating the next frontier, we aim to provide readers with a glimpse into the future trajectory of AI-driven innovations in robotics.

8.2 Cutting-Edge Technologies on the Horizon

As we peer into the future, this section focuses on the cutting-edge technologies that are on the horizon of AI-driven robotics. From quantum computing to bio-inspired robotics, we examine the emerging technologies that have the potential to reshape the landscape. Case studies and prototypes illustrate how these technologies are pushing the boundaries of what is possible, offering a preview of the innovations that may become commonplace in the coming years. By exploring the cutting-edge, we aim to spark curiosity and inspire contemplation about the possibilities that lie ahead.

8.3 Predictions for the Future Landscape

The final section of this chapter ventures into predictions for the future landscape of AI-driven robotics. Drawing insights from industry experts, researchers, and thought leaders, we explore the potential trajectories that the field may follow. From advancements in robot-human collaboration to the integration of AI in everyday life, we paint a picture of the transformative possibilities that await. By synthesizing current trends and extrapolating them into the future, we aim to provide readers with a forward-looking perspective on the evolving role of AI in shaping the landscape of robotic engineering.

This chapter serves as a guide to the potential future trends and emerging technologies in AI-driven robotics. By exploring the next frontier, cutting-edge technologies, and predictions for the future landscape, readers can gain a deeper understanding of the dynamic and evolving nature of the intersection between artificial intelligence and robotic engineering.

9.1 Augmented Intelligence in Collaborative Robotics

The collaboration between humans and AI in robotics marks a paradigm shift in the way we approach automation. In this section, we explore the concept of augmented intelligence, where AI enhances human capabilities rather than replacing them. Through case studies and examples, we delve into the realm of collaborative robotics, where humans and intelligent machines work synergistically to achieve tasks that neither can accomplish alone. Augmented intelligence opens new avenues for productivity, creativity, and efficiency, reshaping the landscape of collaborative efforts in robotic engineering.

9.2 Human-AI Interaction and Interface Design

As humans and AI-powered robots collaborate, the design of interfaces and interaction mechanisms becomes crucial. This section examines the intricacies of human-AI interaction, focusing on interface design that facilitates seamless collaboration. We explore user experience considerations, natural language processing interfaces, and intuitive control systems. Real-world examples showcase how well-designed interfaces enhance communication and cooperation between humans and AI in robotic systems. By understanding the nuances of interaction design, we pave the way for more effective and user-friendly collaborative robotics.

9.3 Training and Skill Development in the AI-Driven Era

The advent of AI-driven robotics necessitates a shift in how individuals acquire and develop skills. This section investigates the training and skill development required in the era of AI. From upskilling the workforce to integrating AI education into curricula, we explore strategies to ensure that individuals are equipped to collaborate effectively with intelligent machines. Case studies highlight successful initiatives and innovative approaches to training, shedding light on how societies can adapt to the changing nature of work and collaboration in the AI-driven era.

This chapter serves as a comprehensive exploration of the collaboration between humans and AI in the field of robotics. By examining augmented intelligence, human-AI interaction, and the evolving landscape of training and skill development, we aim to provide insights into how this collaboration is reshaping industries, job roles, and the very fabric of human-robot interaction.

CHAPTER TEN

Towards a Smarter Tomorrow: Challenges and Opportunities

10.1 Overcoming Technical Challenges

As we embark on the journey towards a smarter tomorrow, we confront a myriad of technical challenges that demand our attention and ingenuity. This section delves into the complexities of overcoming these challenges in the realm of AI-driven robotics. From refining algorithms for increased efficiency to developing more robust hardware, we dissect the intricacies of technological barriers. Through an exploration of real-world cases and emerging solutions, we aim to illuminate the path forward, where innovation and perseverance lead to breakthroughs that propel us into an era of smarter, more capable robotics.

10.2 Addressing Ethical Dilemmas

The evolution of AI in robotics brings forth ethical dilemmas that necessitate careful consideration and proactive solutions. In this section, we navigate through the ethical landscape, addressing issues of fairness, transparency, and the societal impacts of intelligent automation. By examining case studies and engaging in ethical discourse, we aim to foster an awareness that guides the responsible development and deployment of AI-driven robotics. The ethical compass we establish becomes crucial for steering the course toward a smarter tomorrow with due consideration to the societal, cultural, and moral dimensions of innovation.

10.3 Seizing Opportunities for Innovation

In the face of challenges and ethical considerations, opportunities for innovation emerge as beacons of progress. This section explores the proactive steps that can be taken to seize these opportunities, fostering a culture of continuous innovation. From interdisciplinary collaborations that bring fresh perspectives to regulatory frameworks that balance innovation with ethical considerations, we examine strategies that propel the field forward. Real-world examples serve as inspiration, illustrating how seizing opportunities for innovation can lead to transformative advancements, ultimately shaping a future where AI-driven robotics contributes positively to society.

This concluding chapter serves as a call to action, urging stakeholders in the realms of technology, ethics, and innovation to collectively navigate the challenges, address ethical dilemmas, and seize opportunities for innovation. By doing so, we lay the groundwork for a smarter tomorrow a future where AI-driven robotics enhances our lives enriches industries, and contributes to a more intelligent and ethically grounded world.

CONCLUSIONS

11.1 Recap of Key Findings

In this comprehensive exploration of AI-driven innovations in robotic engineering, we have navigated through the historical foundations, current applications, and future trajectories that define the intersection of artificial intelligence and robotics. This section serves as a recapitulation of key findings, distilling the essence of our journey through the evolution, applications, challenges, and opportunities presented in the preceding chapters. By summarizing the key insights, we reinforce the critical elements that have shaped our understanding of this dynamic field.

11.2 Implications for the Future

As we reflect on the insights garnered throughout this book, we turn our gaze toward the implications for the future. This section explores how the current state of AI-driven robotics sets the stage for transformative advancements. What are the potential impacts on industries, economies, and societies at large? How might these technologies shape the way we work, live, and interact? By extrapolating from our findings, we aim to provide readers with a glimpse into the potential futures that may unfold as AI continues to revolutionize robotic engineering.

11.3 Call to Action

The journey through the realms of AI-driven innovations in robotic engineering culminates in a call to action. In this section, we challenge stakeholders—researchers, engineers, policymakers, and enthusiasts—to embrace the responsibilities and opportunities that come with this transformative technology. How can we collectively ensure the responsible and ethical development of AI in robotics? What role can individuals and organizations play in driving positive change? The call to action propels us beyond the pages of this book, urging each reader to be an active participant in shaping the trajectory of AI-driven robotics for a smarter and more sustainable tomorrow.

This concluding chapter not only summarizes our exploration but catalyzes ongoing conversations, initiatives, and collaborative efforts. As we stand on the precipice of a new era of technological advancement, the insights gleaned from this journey provide a foundation for informed decision-making, ethical considerations, and inspired innovation. The call to action resonates with the idea that, collectively, we have the power to shape the future of AI-driven robotics and, in doing so, contribute to a world that leverages technology for the betterment of humanity.